Under the Heavens

Emma J. Swain

BookLeaf
Publishing

Presentation by *BookLeaf Publishing*

Web: www.bookleafpub.com

E-mail: info@bookleafpub.com

ISBN: 9789357740555

First edition 2023

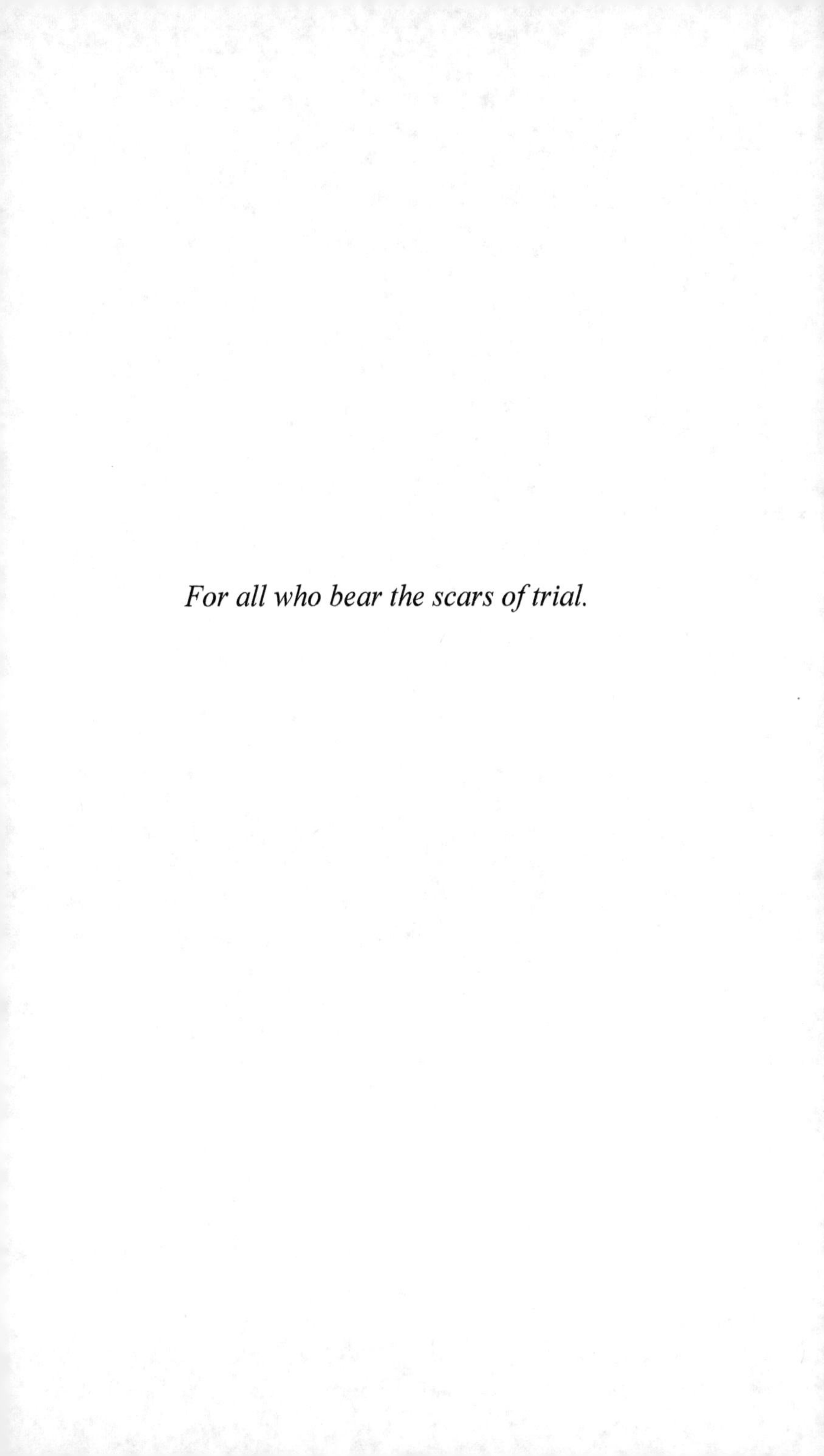

For all who bear the scars of trial.

PREFACE

I can take no credit for this book. The concept was born from Ecclesiastes 3:1-11 and the process of translating this seed of an idea into poetry came from Godly gifting. If these words can touch one person's heart enough to feel a pull towards Him, a yearning to learn about His love, I will have achieved an extremely fulfilling goal.

Seasons are easy to get lost in, to feel as though we are stagnant in our walk through life. My intention with this anthology is to shine a light onto the progression and purpose we cannot see during those times. Although I don't have many years to draw on, I have been through some dark seasons. Equally, I have been blessed with very fruitful seasons. Others have seemed entirely static. Often, we will not be able to see the work God is doing in our lives but through our turbulent roller-coater through life, He remains good, He remains our shepherd and He remains our one constant.

My hope is that this book will emanate that truth and reveal God's love to all those who already know it, those who do not believe it and those who have never encountered it.

It is the reality. God is good.

Dayspring

The break of holy dawn
blooms brightly from on high.
Our eyes are cast upon the gloom
but rise to meet the sacred sign.
With hasty zeal do shadows flee
from glorious light of day,
and banished are the monsters
from peaceful dell and o'er the brae.
Our hearts turn back in praise
for we no more fear those darkened days.
And let no plight of meagre fancy,
ever quell enthusiasm
for the name we've pledged to raise.

Candle in the Dell

My candle flickers on a dripping wick,
casting shadows 'cross pale parchment
as I flex my fingers, purpled,
from the frosty bite of dawn.
The tired nib of quill is quenched
in blackest ink that's fit to mourn.
And as I set about to stain
my hands of solid, fervent grip,
I pause – and ponder all that is,
the enthralling pride of penmanship.

Scrawling tasteful words in haste to
waste away the early hours,
with sounds of rousing dell and lake
wondering where my mind might wake –
Making for the forest thick with elms
and oaks and woodland creatures.
Maybe even twilight ventures
from the bow of skiffs that feature
in my starlit dreams.

Dawn will die and day begins, but
I praise the strength of new-found wings.
My surrendered soul, engraved with words
will humbly work to bless my glen
as told by proxied power of pen.

The Dying Dawn

In the breath before the rising east,
the birdsong calls me from my slumber
to pause upon the chorus
torn asunder
by an awe-struck wonder.

The air so crisp and sky of grey
will carry mists to coat my ley
in wisps of dewy remnant,
brought from night into the risen day.

Heav'n-spilt rays ignite the clouds
that billow by my feet,
and persuades my soul to tarry some
and bathe in morn so sweet.

I'll dwell in bliss of pure design
that draws me to our nearing meet,
and graciously accept the time
before it is complete.

The Risen Day

The wait is ceased.
The mourning clothes are shed.
Stale tears are wiped and bled anew
from crinkled eyes of hope renewed.
A song ensues from hearts alike,
whose silent cries despair their plight,
and have not heard the call of
Child,
upon them as the sun doth smile.
Eyes behold the mottled light
and quench their spirits long deprived
by shadows with their twisted guise.
Fear instils for swift return
to cursèd place where monsters dwell.
But – no more can shackles chafe the wrists
of you in lonely cells,
for though your mind falls pray again,
their hold on you is long expelled.

Planting Season

I kneel in beds of fertile ground.
My fingers trace the enriched soil,
that I have timely blessed despite
your arduous months of earth-bound toil.
Not before this time, I tell you,
would you reap from what I plant.
Allow me now to grant you
what your wait has well preserved.
From my bag of promises, I pull
the seedling thus reserved for you.
In view of harvest plentiful,
a smile becomes my face,
to know you'll turn my blessing back
and pour abounding love on all.
With tears of healing, roots did grow,
and shoots protrude from where I sowed.
The speckled light did warm your face and
turn you t'ward the sun aglow.
In nights of cold and weariness, you
steadfast stole to truths of day,
and never could the frost defile
what refused to bow or sway.
Only by the holy wind
will seedlings catch and fly away,
until they rest in scattered ley

and rise again
in the new day.

Encounter on the Moors

Behold each twisted dryad's home!
sheathed in mossy bed,
who flank the path to heaths
abounding
in grasses soft, to lay my head.

Fearsome is the gale, whose breath does
swirl about mine eyes
and cloud the way to foothold sure,
but wills my soul to skate on tides
of wind and ruthless, wily moor.

Gaze upon the brook whose
power tempts you to its waters.
While on its surface skims
the frosted pebbles, unabating,
the courage of your heart debating
the author of its true creating.

The Journey

I walk down paths of distant promise,
yearning for wildflowers
growing loftily o'er yonder.
I wish for cobbled stone on which
to place my feet
with thoughts of wander.

I thirst for barren springs
and hunger after fruitless trees.
I dream for beds of heather smooth
to rest whene'er the thought does please.

I cry from cold and curse the pain
I'm saddled with till journey's end.
And yet I clutch the burden tight
believing joy, on it, depends.

But when I cut its fearsome ties,
my heart is lightened by the sight
of warming hearth with air so rich –
my spirit kindled firelight.

So brightly is its bloom
that it does cast a glow upon my road
revealing in iridescent plumes,

provision thus bestowed.

Looming oaks of splendid stature
set my course from tempts to sway
and have ensured my blessed shade
from which no flower could dissuade.

Carpets of sweet-smelling grass
have soothed my feet in stride,
and tell me of the graciousness
of my beloved guide.

Mountain Perspective

My feet remain on solid ground
yet my head does graze the heavens.
Ablaze with fiery zeal, unbound,
I'm left with fervent, awed impression.
Confounded by the whispered questions,
glistening on an untamed breeze,
I bristle in sublimity,
which all my senses firmly seize.
The mind cannot fathom.
All hearts are appeased,
as unrelenting splendour grants
permission for a peace-filled ease.
Significances
of my past
will dwindle into dust,
for this zealot fire abreast,
has kindled breath and immense trust.
I cry myself to barren ashes
and watch as thunder strikes
my heart of molten frivolity
and moulds it into light.
And so I bask,
as duly called,
in might of sovereign thus residing
no longer in the cloudy skies,
but lives behind unblinded eyes.

Basking in the Presence

I'm on my knees –
arms outstretched
to grasp at curling tendrils of
your spirit-rich, embalming air.

I call on you
and tears fall from eyes
into my humble smile
of thanks
and whispered prayer
that keeps me from
a dark despair.

I am stilled.

I listen.

Every thought intersecting
the way to you
is silenced.
My mind hushes
to hear your whisper
and rushes to meet
the words you deliver.

Reality greets my
opened eyes
but my heart still throbs
from fresh release
of worldly ties.

Noontide

My golden constant is at its peak,
telling of the laborious works
complete and thriving in midday heat.
It tells of hours left to strive, but
despite my foe's contriving will,
it hasn't met will of He
whose purposes fulfil.
I endeavour still to try,
revealing that which veils in guise –
the parasite who leeches light
until the tragic time of cruel demise.
I face the choice at morning's end
to flee pursuing shadows,
and run the abyss
with no protection to defend.
Or do I stride towards my call
– that's sure to lure the monsters close –
and trust in truth of firm set values,
in which I've learnt supplies the most.
No sword of vengeance do I wield,
just simple might that's meekly stout,
my stronghold and
my valiant Shield.

Lull of the Lily

Vastly do the grounds beneath my feet
stretch onward bound,
and yet, I stay, unmoving,
as I plead for certain sign or sound.
With grasses grown
and paths unclear,
every sordid tempting
now distracts from where
I once drew near.
And though the lily
does not wait
to bloom and burst in rosy hue,
her intricacies, still at work,
appear to us as bided time,
until its blossom's thusly due.
Through the lovely patience
of her crimson, peeling petals,
exalting is she, at the time,
when pressure tested for her mettle.
And so I fix my gaze upon
the works of heaven still ongoing,
hidden to my shallow eyes.
Like the lily, ever growing,
I hold steadfast until my promise
delivers me from darken'd skies.

Reap Day

15

The barren fields of barley that sought
mourning tears to water,
now sprouts its golden plaited heads,
and calls for pearly grains to shed.
As each seedling first was sowed,
in plentiful array,
the harvest gleaned is bountiful;
its faith is blessed upon reap day.
Yonder in my neighbour field,
the crop is sparse and sheaves are drooping.
due to poorly planted seeds
their harvest thus is poorly granting.
And so I share the yield of mine
and teach my neighbour how to sow.
When next the reap day comes about
they'll bask in harvest overflow.

Golden Hour

Curling amber ornaments that dot
the autumn trees,
with gilded, bending beams
it seems
a mystic match
for gold-tipped dreams.

It glints off wings and pearly rings
that ripple under scrutiny.
Changing commonplace
to beauty,
as it's necessary duty,
in the honeyed lens
of euphony.

An ample glow will
freckle faces
turning t'ward its source's
grace and
dapple that which wouldn't flower,
if not for Autumn's
golden hour.

Till the Fire Dies

Hearthside peace induces all my
worldly qualms to cease.
It calms unrested thought's increasing
tendency to fly
upon the given wings of mind
that skate the springs and cloudy sky.

Tendrils tipped in orange glow
will tickle at the nearing eve,
with spirited and fervent flickers
licking at the browning wood from
kindler's wicker weave.

Spitting out its embers
that flap t'ward the dusty stars and
shrouded by the pluming smoke and
ash the ground revokes.

Sparks that burst and shower down
their snowy flakes of cinder, warming
hearth and hand and black'ning timber
stored away from depths of winter.

Ever causing brightened eyes
to entrancingly now to linger
till the fire dies.

The Rescue

Kingdom spirit
let me glide on
silvered lines
of angel arms
and lift me
over water's edge
to dredge up
poor lost souls
from blacken'd depths
of misery.

Kingdom spirit
pull the tide
to bob beneath
their heads
and hold them up
on feathered wings
and raise their
stolen voices
up to sing.

Kingdom spirit
onward fly with
rescued children
now in keep.

And light the way
for us to find
your
little, lost
afflicted sheep.

Vigil at Dusk

The sky appears to fall
in tandem with the sun,
as it sinks toward a westward slumber,
shun of darkness now is done.
With cricket chorus tuning
for a night of silent humming,
my beating heart grows restless
for the dangers soon forthcoming.
I lapse into a pleading mutter, as the
stuttering of breath does shudder
at the shadows curling t'ward
the sheath of my diminished sword.
O reignite my dying lantern
so I might sleep in fearless peace,
or warn me now with certainty
and from all hopes I'll be released.
Into the cooling air of dusk
these words begin to echo,
until a light breaks forth from yonder
clearing o'er the meadow.
In radiant bursts, the glow is scattered
till in amber I am showered
with unequalled iridescence,
filling me with heav'nly presence.
With glorious vigour I do rejoice, for

He knew my fears and heard my cries.
Amidst my plight of shadows nigh,
my father sends me fireflies.

Twilit Observations

Residual light will ebb,
as its twilit encore scalds the earth,
from which, its glowering beams are led,
and from our hillside, now have fled.

Evening birdsong thus ensues
from dimly prompting skies,
and though the distant song will fade
come morning, it will rise.

The silhouetted statues,
whose branches flank both path and road
are painted in the canvas sky,
as oil-stained figures of nature's ode.

Sweet sundown air meets flushed-pink skin,
and soothes the crying babe.
As all are plunged into the night,
it sweeps fresh blessing 'cross the glade.

The Ebb Tide

The water reels,
calling back its pearly rings
all the while, its pressure stings
the skin of limbs held captive
while they're clipped of saving wings.

Ripples rising.
The figure submerges,
leaving light to be purged from
a sky growing dimmer,
dappled by a descending sun's glimmer.

And though the pain is sharply felt,
their eyes are blinded
from the melting waters closing tightly
overhead.

Into the depths they're fiercely pulled
until their grasp on truth is dulled
to soak in waters, thick with lies,
and drift in wake of muffled cries.

Talons

They have her heart.
Wingèd beasts with
poised, hooked claws.
Piercing flesh with
taunts that graze
the skin of her beliefs.
A tear slips
from her eye
as it does with mine to see
how they toy with
her misery.
Everyday I watch
them as they
etch the poison
further in,
working with their
twinning grins,
believing that I cannot win.
She doesn't know
how far she's fallen
and where she ought to be.
But someday, child,
I promise this,
you will come back to me.

The Place Where Monsters Dwell

I wear a mask of half emotion,
and veil the currents of
tormenting thoughts and thick delusion,
aiding in this bleak confusion.

I know this place,
I know it all too well,
for I'm in the place where monsters dwell.
Every time I wish the last
and yet my past won't let me quell
the thoughts that only demons tell.

There is no sound in dead of night
and raging are the voices' shouts
with an agency I have endowed,
they echo in my head of thunderous clouds.

I beg of lapping waves o'erhead,
they not condemn my mind to tread
the darkened waters, groping souls.
Whate'er the price to walk on land,
I tell them I will pay their twisted toll
and bear my blistered brand.

I wait in my windowless cell,
no concept of time or meaning or truth.
I trace every mark from each capture renewed,
engraving once more as my rescue grows distant
and as the days darken,
it further eludes.

Sunrise

Light bursts
amid the darkened mountain plains
and stains the snowy peaks
until all before me turns to gold.
My saving rays bleed into night,
unfolding as they spill and curl
in mystic plumes,
to drive back the dark
and let His splendid glory bloom.
Among the blessed chorus
of angelic awe and praise,
I see my Lord as dressed in light;
for him alone my hands will raise.
For I know that
He who parts the seas
will part them for my wand'ring soul.
And He who moves the mountains
will move them for my mind made whole.
So with new breath to fill my lungs
this broken body is reborn,
and all creation turns to awe
the break of holy dawn.